HEAVEN'S SOUL CLEANSE

HEAVEN'S SOUL CLEANSE

30 DAYS OF HIS GLORY

FELIX HALPERN

It's Supernatural! Press and Messianic Vision, Inc.

Cover and interior by Terry Clifton

ISBN 13 TP: 978-0-7684-6197-8

ISBN 13 eBook: 978-0-7684-6198-5

For Worldwide Distribution, Printed in the U.S.A.

1 2 3 4 5 6 7 8 / 25 24 23 22 21

CONTENTS

PREFACE

Heaven's Soul Cleanse is a passionate pursuit of God that will reboot your spiritual life and launch you into a heavenly operating system. As you journey through these thirty days, your soul will be submerged under the anointing of a select portion of Psalms purposely designed to cleanse your soul.

The only requirement?

Give thirty days in complete adoration of God. Get ready for an adventure.

INTRODUCTION

THERE IS A CALL TO ACTION THAT COMES TO every heart that embarks upon this journey.

But will you make it through? Not everyone will!

By way of background, and how I received the Heavenly Soul Cleanse, is important, because it came from heaven.

In September of 2019, from a doctor mis-prescribing an incorrect dosage of medication, my body ingested 7½ months of medication in less than a month. This kind of overdose can cause coma, instant death, and/or cardiac arrest. I experienced the latter.

Then, just like slipping out of a room, my spirit slipped out of my body and I was transported into the third heaven; my circle of life came to an end, my dead body was on the couch, and I knew I had crossed over.

The full accounting of this is provided in an additional writing called, *A Rabbi's Journey to Heaven.* Offered exclusively by Sid Roth ministries.

But upon my return I was given an extraordinary gift that you must get ready for! Not only is it entirely based upon the Word of God, it will open the sky over your life, and you will no longer feel like you're living under the confinements of a ceiling. You will discover an intrinsically new spiritual routine focused entirely upon the adoration of God.

Each one that undertakes this journey will understand the meaning of transformation, as your soul is set free from the weight of earthly things.

You see, I don't know when I realized the air down here was getting stifling, but within the first three days of my return, God eradicated what I call the *transactional prayer life* that characterizes most of church culture, and now I live in a *transformational prayer life*, or a *sufficiency mindset,* every morning of every day.

THE BOOK OF PSALMS

Upon my return, I was directed by God to immerse myself in this one book for a season: the book of Psalms. That season would last not three days, three weeks or months, but over a year now and counting. Although God gave us sixty-six books in the Bible to learn from, this one particular book has over 200 verses that focus upon the magnification and enlargement of God. Almost 50% of the entire book focuses upon His Glory.

For example, Psalm 8, like many of the psalms provided here, is called the song of the Astronomer according to some ancient writers: A perfect context for these glory psalms. You, I believe, will feel like one when you are finished. Psalm 8, is a sweet song of admiration.[1]

Here you will experience your soul lifted as you detach from the world. You will feel withdrawn from the earth, and rise to lofty mysteries from out of our human anxieties. The mind abandons itself to unexplored glory. Nature becomes

---

1   *The Treasury of David*/Spurgeon/Hendrickson Publishing

seen in wonderful simplicity and sees God's wisdom and majesty throughout.

Psalms also speaks more about the soul than any other book of the Bible. If we need to understand the relationship between our soul and spirit, then the book of Psalms is the place to turn.

Over the course of that time, particularly within the first 30 days, the Father showed me how the top could come off my life through *transformational prayer*. It felt like spiritual arteries opening up, then branching out into my daily life.

I realized that we can go through the course of our lives, and, figuratively speaking, pass the bush without seeing the fire in it. Many of us are satisfied to go through life not stopping for more of Him. You know, to stop and say *"Hineni*—here I am."

Well, ever since September of 2019, I can't wait to get before the Lord in prayer every morning. I feel I can see for miles. I look up and finally sense a sky overhead, and no longer a roof.

In other words, my days feel limitless. I pray, and I leave my needs with my Heavenly Father.

You see, I have learned the art of detachment! I truly found the secret ingredient that makes "His" yoke easy and my burdens light. No longer do I need to repeatedly pray the same thing because my prayers and burdens have moved from transactional to transformational. Essentially, I changed ownership.

BUT AGAIN, WHAT ABOUT MY BURDENS?

Surely, earth is hard, and heaven is easy. As I noted, earth is a need-based environment. At the end of 2019 began COVID-19. Several years back it was the real estate collapse and the Great Recession. Personal needs in our life visit us daily, weekly, and monthly. Prayers needs run the gamut.

We pray for our children, grandchildren, the needs of the church, society, government, and our ministries. The list has no end, and our answered prayers today will only be replaced with new ones tomorrow. I cannot remember when I was without multiple prayer needs at any one given time.

So, yes, burdens come.

We also tell people to cast them upon the Lord and we should. In Psalm 55:22 it states, "Cast your burden on the Lord, *and He shall sustain you;* He shall never permit the righteous to be moved" (NKJV). Notice the promise to be sustained and be unmoved.

Then in the Book of Matthew 11:28-29 it says, "Come to me, all you who are weary and burdened, and *I will give you rest.* Take my yoke upon you and learn from me, for I am gentle and humble in heart, and *you will find rest for your souls."*

Paul pens a letter to the Colossians in chapter 3:2. "Therefore, since you have been raised with Christ, strive for the things above, where Christ is seated at the right hand of God. *Set your minds on things above, not on earthly things"* (Berean Study Bible).

But no one has told us how to accomplish it in our daily life without continual discipline and control over our thoughts.

We also have these words in Philippians 4:6-7, "Be anxious for nothing, but in everything by prayer and supplication, with thanksgiving, let your requests be made known to God; and the peace of God, which surpasses all understanding, will guard your hearts and minds through Christ Jesus" (NKJV). *Notice the promise of a peace that surpasses all understanding.*

Yet, given the power of the blood of Messiah and His sacrifice, many people have their burdens return like a boomerang and unrest settles into their soul again.

Does this sound familiar?

Imagine the lifting of your spirit when your soul is set free from need during need; this is called a miracle. It is called the power of God—the glory of God—the powerful grace of God. Complaining and worrying flee.

Obsessiveness over the future and the COVID-19 virus flee. Your soul is drawn upward and your mind becomes fixed on heavenly things—the majesty and grandeur of God. It feels like the temporal atmosphere has been lifted.

Friend, I may sound idealistic, but I am here to tell you it's possible with some simple steps. You also don't have to suffer a heart attack, die, and return as I did. As I received this gift, I offer it to you. And I will show you how to be free of your burdens in a way that is sustainable and without extraneous effort or mental discipline. But to get there, we must first overcome some lines of conflict.

THE BIG QUESTION.

The question is: Is God big enough to sustain your losses and pressures for one month?

Are you willing to change the ownership of your needs and burdens?

Of course, you will say, "yes."

But, truly and genuinely, are you willing to drown your needs and starve your soul of the natural and earthly order for just one month? Putting it another way: Are you willing to take a vacation from your prayer needs for one month, and allow your Father to keep them for you, for a season?

ACCEPTING THE MISSION

If you choose to accept this mission, you will follow in the words of the psalmist in 96:7-8, and "ascribe to the Lord glory and strength. Ascribe to the Lord the glory due to his name."

Go ahead, try giving the Lord only glory in your prayer time with no petition, praise, thanksgiving, or intercession. Try it for a day, two, and then for seven, and experience its awkwardness.

Why does this feel awkward?

Because as I have maintained, we have been indoctrinated into a transactional prayer life rather than one that is transformational. Therefore, we live in an insufficiency mindset rather than one of sufficiency. This is where transactional prayer life is rooted.

Transformational prayer is not static because it is service minded. You see, the more we detach from our needs, the greater capacity we have to serve God and others, because it is sacrificial and continues to orient our soul toward heaven.

The truth of this is sharply highlighted when we become more spiritually and heavenly minded, and our prayers are no longer as barnacles on a ship slowing us down. We suddenly have more time to exalt our God in heaven.

FORMULA AND SCALE

From yet another perspective, we have the issue of scale, which also goes to heart of our secret ingredient prayer life.

In my experience as a believer for over 45 years, and serving in ministry for more than 30 years, 75% of one's prayer life is spent in the transactional space trying to move the hand of God. Remember, like the prayer for the Lord to heal, help, do, give, etc.

This is not to say that there is something wrong with transactional prayer. It is just that this kind of prayer is the predominant space in our prayer culture. Possibly, the fact that we seem to emphasize this type of prayer speaks of the culture in which we live as well.

Returning to our topic.

I would predict that only 25% of prayer is in the exaltation prayer space. But the first is likely higher than 75% and the second is lower than 25%. Unless there is a structural adjustment in this formula, we will remain a in need-based prayer life and never live under a higher atmosphere.

Making the Adjustment

What if, and just what if, we reversed the formula?

What if 75% of our prayer life was in the magnification and exaltation space, and 25% was in the need or transactional space?

Can you imagine the effect upon your relationship with the Lord, and its rejuvenation of your soul?

This, my friend, is the purpose of the 30 Days in His Glory. Your soul will be cleansed and a new operating system will ensue in your prayer life. Essentially, it is the launch vehicle to get you into the atmosphere of heaven.

A Healthy Launch

During the 30 days of magnifying and enlarging God, don't worry about hearing from Him. In the process, God will speak to you, so have a journal ready. But remember, this is a time of complete exaltation, adoration, and enlargement of our heavenly Father.

Get ready to swim in the river of God! It's all about healing your soul, bringing it into greater submission to the Spirit, and entering upon a higher plane of heavenly living.

The psalms in this book will help you with this. You will catch the rhythm of praying words of exaltation and magnification, and it will become like second nature. You may also choose to highlight them in your own Bible. You can then open your Bible anywhere and meditate upon these verses or take this small book with you. I have been in the Psalms for over 12 months, and they still consume me daily.

WHAT TIME IS BEST?

I've found that spending time with the Lord first thing in the morning seems to yield the best results for my day.

"Why?" do you ask?

The morning is when all is calm and quiet. When our surroundings are quiet, it is easier for our minds and souls to follow, which is the opportune time to allow the Lord to speak. Here is what the Bible reveals about the mornings:

> *Let me hear in the morning of your steadfast love, for in you I trust. Make me know the way I should go, for to you I lift up my soul* (Psalm 143:8 ESV).

> *I will sing of your strength; I will sing aloud of your steadfast love in the morning. For you have been to me a fortress and a refuge in the day of my distress* (Psalm 59:16 ESV).

> *But I, O Lord, cry to you; in the morning, my prayer comes before you* (Psalm 88:13 ESV).

> *Satisfy us in the morning with your steadfast love that we may rejoice and be glad all our days* (Psalm 90:14 ESV).

> *I rise before dawn and cry for help; I have put my hope in your words* (Psalm 119:47 ESV).

If you are willing to commit every morning for 30 days to the Lord, He will begin to absorb you, and you will start to absorb Him. You will reboot your spiritual system, and your soul will come into daily alignment with the atmosphere of the heavens.

FINAL INSTRUCTIONS

Each morning begins ONLY with elevation psalms. Pray these psalms as your own; it is important to personalize them because you are praying them back to your Heavenly Father.

As you begin, if you have the urge to ask God for something, STOP! Catch yourself and start again. In the beginning it will feel awkward.

During this time, restrain yourself from petition, praise, or giving thanks. This is a time of complete exaltation, adoration, and enlargement of our heavenly Father. Like a liver cleanse, or any cleansing of the body, a specific regimen must be followed for a set period to achieve its goal of this Heavenly Soul Cleanse. For 30 days your time with the Lord will be as the following:

> *You, oh Lord, the Maker of Heaven and earth, the steward of life, the*

Creator and sustainer of all. Without You, there would be nothing. Without You, the earth would be dark and lifeless. You, Father, are perfect and holy, forgiving, compassionate. Always, Lord, you are slow to anger and quick to forgive.

An Important Note: Transformation or elevation prayers are absent of I, me, us, my mine, or we.

Who do you see?

Your Father.

Thirty days of this? Wow!

Get ready to swim in the river of God! Remember, it's all about healing your soul and entering upon a higher plane of peaceful living.

Press through it!

REVIEW THE FOLLOWING:

A. Praise is "I" centered. We are always thanking Him for what He has done for me and us. This is not the time for that. At least for the next 30 days.

B. Petition is "I" centered. "Lord, please help me, deliver us, and alleviate my situation." Again, this is not the time for that. At least for the next 30 days.

C. Glory psalms are "God" centered. "Lord, You are glorious and majestic in all your ways." "You set the stars in place and call them by name." "From day unto day, and night unto night, You are there." "From eternities past to the eternities that await Your creation, You shall always be upon your glorious throne." "Nothing compares to Your greatness."

D. Begin at the same time every morning. Whatever time you are accustomed to spending with God, end it for the day. *Do no further reading for the day. Allow the Word to wash over you.*

E. After three days or so, you will begin to sense a different perception of your day. God, the Creator, will start to permeate your mind. You will be more perceptive to His handprint everywhere.

F. Remember, for 30 days, you will only be magnifying and enlarging God by praying elevation and magnification psalms.

G. As you catch the rhythm, and as noted earlier, speak these back to Him as your personal prayers. Let your meditations flow from your lips to magnify and elevate God during this time. It may take a week or so to get a heavenly rhythm, but press through!

H. When you are set free and have entered the transformational space with God, help someone else get set free!

Should you take on this mission, the psalmist words will penetrate your soul and saturate your mind. The Spirit of God will give you a new vocabulary. You will become, as the psalmist states in 45:2, "I address my verses to the king, my tongue is like the pen of a ready scribe" (ESV).

HANDBOOK OF
THE SOUL

Before you begin this Heavenly Soul Cleanse, pray the two preparatory prayers of the words of the Apostle Paul that follow. Important words have been highlighted, with liberty taken for certain emphasis. These prayers will be the last petitions and requests that you make before you begin the 30 days in His Glory Meditation.

PAUL'S PRAYERS

I pray that the FATHER of GLORY, the GOD of my LORD JESUS the MESSIAH, would IMPART to me the RICHES of the SPIRIT of WISDOM and the SPIRIT of REVELATION to KNOW HIM through my DEEPEN- ING INTIMACY with Him.

I pray that the LIGHT of GOD will illuminate the eyes of my imagination (INNERMOST BEING), FLOODING me with LIGHT, UNTIL I experi- ence the FULL REVELATION of the FUTURE to which He is calling me to.

I pray that I will CONTINUALLY EXPERIENCE the IMMEASUR- ABLE GREATNESS of GOD'S

POWER made available to me THROUGH FAITH. Then my LIFE will be an ADVERTISEMENT of this IMMENSE POWER as it works through me!

This is the SAME mighty power that was released when GOD raised MESSIAH from the dead and (SEATED Him) EXALTED Him to the place of HIGHEST HONOR and SUPREME AUTHORITY in the heavenly realm! And He raised me up together with Him [when I believed], and giving me the position of an adopted heir of His GLORY, and seating me with Him in the heavenly places, [because I am] in Messiah Jesus.

EPHESIANS 3:16-20 (TPT)

...I pray that GOD would unveil WITHIN me the UNLIMITED RICHES of His GLORY and FAVOR until HIS SUPERNAT-URAL STRENGTH floods my INNERMOST BEING.

...I pray for HIS DIVINE MIGHT and EXPLOSIVE POWER....to CON-STANTLY use MY FAITH, and that the LIFE of MESSIAH will be released deep INSIDE me.

...I pray that the resting place of HIS LOVE will become the very SOURCE and ROOT of my LIFE. THEN I will be empowered to discover what every child of God experiences—the Great Magnitude of the ASTON-ISHING LOVE of MESSIAH in all its dimensions.

That it is deeply intimate and far-reaching, Enduring and Inclu-sive of all of His GOODNESS. That

HIS ENDLESS LOVE is BEYOND MEASUREMENT and Transcends my Understanding.

This EXTRAVAGANT LOVE pours INTO me UNTIL I am FILLED TO OVERFLOWING with the FULL-NESS of GOD! I WILL NOT DOUBT GOD'S MIGHTY POWER to WORK IN me now in order to accomplish ALL that I am about to receive.

He and He alone will achieve INFINITELY MORE than my GREAT-EST REQUEST; my MOST UNBE-LIEVABLE DREAM that EXCEEDS my WILDEST IMAGINATION!

GOD, YOU will OUTDO THEM ALL, BY YOUR MIRACULOUS POWER that CONSTANTLY ENERGIZES me.

PSALMS

PSALM 8:1-2 (AMP AND NLT)

O LORD, my LORD, Your majestic NAME FILLS the earth!

Your GLORY [the Radiance of Your Presence] is HIGHER than the heavens.

Out of the mouths of infants and nursing babes You have established strength (Matthew 21:16 translates that word "PRAISE") because of my adversaries,

That I might SILENCE THE ENEMY [through PRAISE] and make the revengeful CEASE.

PSALM 8:3-9 (AMP)

When I see and consider Your heavens, the work of Your fingers, the moon and the stars, which You have established,

What am I that You are mindful of me,

As the son of an [earthborn] man that You care for me? Yet You have made me a little lower than GOD, and You have crowned me with GLORY and honor.

You made me to have DOMINION over the works of Your hands; You have put ALL things under my feet, All sheep and oxen, and also the beasts of the field,

The birds of the air, and the fish of the sea, whatever passes through the paths of the seas.

O LORD, my LORD, how MAJESTIC and GLORIOUS and EXCELLENT is Your NAME in ALL the EARTH!

Psalm 9:1-11 (AMP)

I will give thanks and praise the LORD, with ALL my heart; I will tell ALOUD all Your WONDERS and MARVELOUS DEEDS. I will rejoice and exult IN You;

I will sing PRAISE to Your NAME, O MOST HIGH.

When MY ENEMIES turn back, they STUMBLE and PERISH before You.

For You have maintained my RIGHT and my CAUSE; You have sat on the throne JUDGING RIGHTEOUSLY. You have rebuked the nations, You have destroyed the wicked and unrepentant; You have wiped out their name forever and ever.

The ENEMY has been CUT OFF and has VANISHED in EVERLASTING ruins,

You have uprooted their cities; the very memory of them has perished.

But the You, LORD will remain and sit ENTHRONED FOREVER; He has prepared and established His throne for JUDGMENT. And He will JUDGE the world in RIGHTEOUSNESS; He will execute JUDGMENT for the nations with FAIRNESS.

The Lord also will be a REFUGE and a STRONGHOLD for the OPPRESSED,

A REFUGE in times of trouble; and those who know Your NAME [who have experienced Your PRECIOUS MERCY] will put their CONFIDENT TRUST in You, for You, O LORD, have not abandoned those who seek You.

I sing PRAISES to the LORD, who dwells in Zion; I DECLARE among the peoples Your [GREAT and WONDROUS] DEEDS.

PSALM 10:16-18 (AMP)

The LORD is KING FOREVER and EVER; the nations will perish from Your land.

O LORD, You have heard the desire of the humble and oppressed; You will strengthen my heart, and You will incline Your ear to hear,

You will VINDICATE and OBTAIN JUSTICE for the fatherless and the oppressed, so that man who is of the earth will no longer terrify them.

PSALM 11:3-7 (AMP)

If the foundations [of a godly society] are destroyed, what can the righteous do?

The LORD is in His Holy temple; the LORD'S throne is in Heaven. His eyes see, His eyelids test the children of men.

The LORD tests the righteous and the wicked, and His soul hates the one who loves violence. Upon the wicked god-less) He will rain coals of fire;

Fire and brimstone and a dreadful scorching wind will be the portion of their cup [of doom].

For the LORD is [ABSOLUTELY] RIGHTEOUS, HE LOVES RIGH-TEOUSNESS (VIRTUE, MORALITY, JUSTICE); since I am upright I shall see Your FACE.

PSALM 18:1-36 (NLT)

I love You, LORD; You are my strength.

The LORD is my ROCK, my FOR-TRESS, and my SAVIOR; my GOD is my ROCK in whom I find PROTEC-TION. He is my SHIELD, the power that SAVES me, and my PLACE of SAFETY.

I called on the LORD, who is WOR-THY of PRAISE, and He SAVED me from my ENEMIES. The ropes of death entangled me; floods of destruc-tion swept over me.

The grave wrapped its ropes around me; death laid a trap in my path.

But in my distress I cried out to the LORD; yes, I prayed to my GOD for help.

He heard me from His sanctuary; my cry to Him reached His ears.

Then the earth quaked and trembled.

The foundations of the mountains shook; they quaked because of His anger. Smoke poured from His nostrils; fierce flames leaped from His mouth. Glowing coals blazed forth from Him.

He opened the heavens and came down; dark storm clouds were beneath His feet.

Mounted on a mighty angelic being, He flew, soaring on the wings of the wind.

He shrouded Himself in darkness,

veiling His approach with dark rain clouds.

Thick clouds shielded the brightness around Him and rained down hail and burning coals.

The LORD thundered from heaven;

the voice of the Most High resounded

amid the hail and burning coals. He SHOT His ARROWS and SCATTERED His ENEMIES; great bolts of lightning flashed, and they were CONFUSED.

Then at Your command, O LORD,

at the blast of Your breath, the bottom of the sea could be seen, and the foundations of the earth were laid bare.

He reached down from heaven and RESCUED ME; He drew me out of deep waters. He RESCUED me from my powerful enemies, from those who hated me and were too strong for me.

They attacked me at a moment when I was in distress, but the LORD supported me.

He led me to a PLACE of SAFETY; He RESCUED ME because He DELIGHTS in me. The LORD rewarded me for doing right; He RESTORED me because of my innocence. For I have kept the ways of the LORD; I have not turned from my GOD to follow evil.

I have followed all His regulations;
I have never abandoned His decrees.
I am blameless before GOD;
I have kept myself from sin.

The LORD rewarded me for doing right.

He has seen my innocence.

To the faithful You show Yourself FAITHFUL; to those with integrity You show INTEGRITY. To the pure You show Yourself PURE, but to the crooked You show Yourself shrewd.

You RESCUE the HUMBLE, but You humiliate the proud. You light a lamp for me. The LORD, my GOD, lights up my darkness. IN YOUR STRENGTH I can crush an army; with my GOD I can scale any wall.

GOD'S WAY is PERFECT. ALL the LORD'S PROMISES prove TRUE.

He is a SHIELD for all who LOOK to HIM FOR PROTECTION.

For who is GOD except the Lord?

Who but my GOD is a SOLID ROCK?

GOD arms me with strength, and He MAKES MY WAY PERFECT. He makes me as SUREFOOTED as a deer, enabling me to stand on mountain heights.

He trains my hands for battle; He strengthens my arm to draw a bronze bow.

You have given me YOUR SHIELD of VICTORY. Your right hand supports me;

Your help has made me great. You have made a WIDE PATH for my feet to keep them from slipping.

PSALM 19:1-11 (AMP)

The heavens are telling of the GLORY of GOD; And the expanse [of heaven] is declaring the work of His hands.

Day after day they pour forth speech, night after night they reveal knowledge.

There is no speech, nor are there [spoken] words [from the stars]; their voice is not heard. Yet their voice [in quiet evidence] has gone out through all the earth,

Their words to the end of the world.

In them and in the heavens, He has made a tent for the sun, which is as a bridegroom coming out of his chamber; it rejoices as a strong man to run his course.

The sun's rising is from one end of the heavens, and its circuit to the other end of them; There is nothing hidden from its heat.

The LAW of the LORD is PERFECT (FLAWLESS), RESTORING and REFRESHING the SOUL;

The STATUTES of the LORD are RELIABLE and TRUSTWORTHY, making WISE the simple. The PRE-CEPTS of the LORD are RIGHT, bringing JOY to the HEART;

The COMMANDMENT of the LORD is PURE, ENLIGHTENING the EYES.

The FEAR of the LORD is CLEAN, ENDURING FOREVER; The JUDG-MENTS of the LORD are TRUE, they are RIGHTEOUS ALTOGETHER.

They are more DESIRABLE than gold, yes, than much fine gold; SWEETER also than honey and the drippings of the honeycomb. Moreover, by them Your servant is WARNED [REMINDED, ILLUMINATED, and INSTRUCTED];

In keeping them I have a GREAT REWARD.

PSALM 24 (AMP)

The earth is the LORD'S, and the fullness of it, the world, and those who dwell in it. For He has founded it upon the seas, and established it upon the streams and the rivers.

Who may ascend onto the mountain of the LORD? And who may stand in His Holy Place? He who has CLEAN HANDS and a PURE HEART, who has not lifted up his soul to what is false, nor has sworn [oaths] deceitfully.

He shall receive a blessing from the LORD, and righteousness from the GOD of his SALVATION. This is the generation (description) of those who DILIGENTLY SEEK HIM and REQUIRE HIM as their GREATEST NEED, who seek Your FACE, even [as did] Jacob.

Lift up your heads, O gates, and be lifted up, ancient doors, that the KING of GLORY may come in. Who is the KING of GLORY? The LORD STRONG and MIGHTY, the LORD MIGHTY in BATTLE.

Lift up your heads, O gates, and lift them up, ancient doors, that the KING of GLORY may come in. Who is [He then] this KING of GLORY? The LORD of HOSTS(OF HEAVEN'S ARMIES),

He is the KING of GLORY [who RULES over ALL creation with His HEAVENLY ARMIES].

PSALM 25:8-10 (AMP)

GOOD and UPRIGHT is the LORD;
Therefore, He instructs sinners in the way.

He leads the HUMBLE in JUSTICE,

Psalm 29 (AMP)

PRAISE the LORD, O sons of the MIGHTY, PRAISE to the LORD for His GLORY and STRENGTH. PRAISE to the LORD the GLORY due His NAME; Worship the Lord in the BEAUTY and MAJESTY of His HOLINESS [as the CREATOR and source of HOLINESS].

The VOICE of the LORD is upon the waters; The GOD of GLORY thunders;

The LORD is over many waters.

The VOICE of the LORD is POWERFUL; The VOICE of the LORD is FULL of MAJESTY.

The VOICE of the LORD breaks the cedars. Yes, the LORD breaks in pieces the cedars of Lebanon. He makes Lebanon skip like a calf, and Mount Hermon like a young, wild ox.

The VOICE of the LORD rakes flames of fire (lightning). The VOICE of the

LORD shakes the wilderness; The LORD shakes the wilderness of Kadesh.

The VOICE of the LORD makes the doe labor and give birth and strips the forests bare; all in HIS TEMPLE SAY "GLORY!"

The LORD sat as KING over the flood;

Yes, the LORD sits as KING FOREVER.

The LORD will give [UNYIELDING and IMPENETRABLE] STRENGTH to me;

The LORD will bless me with PEACE.

PSALM 31:19-20 (AMP)

How GREAT is Your GOODNESS,

Which You have stored up for those who [REVERENTLY] FEAR You, which You have prepared for those who take REFUGE in You!

In the SECRET PLACE of Your PRESENCE, You HIDE me from the plots and conspiracies of man; You keep me secretly in a shelter (pavilion) from the strife of tongues.

PSALM 33:10-22 (AMP)

The LORD nullifies the counsel of the nations; And makes the thoughts and plans of the people ineffective.

The COUNSEL of the LORD stands FOREVER, and thoughts and plans of His heart endure through all generations. Blessed [fortunate, prosperous, and favored by GOD] is the nation whose GOD is the LORD, the people whom He has chosen as His own inheritance.

The LORD looks [down] from heaven;

He sees all the sons of man; from His dwelling place He looks closely

Upon all the inhabitants of the earth—

He who fashions the hearts of them all, considers and understands all that they do.

The king is not saved by the great size of his army; A warrior is not rescued by his great strength. A horse is a false hope for victory; nor does it deliver anyone by its great strength.

Behold, the EYE of the LORD is upon them that FEAR HIM [and WORSHIP Him with AWE-INSPIRED REVERENCE and OBEDIENCE],

I hope [CONFIDENTLY] in Your COMPASSION and LOVING KINDNESS, O LORD.

YOU RESCUE my life FROM DEATH and keep me ALIVE in FAMINE. I WAIT [EXPECTANTLY] for the LORD;

He is my HELP and SHIELD.

IN HIM my HEART REJOICES, Because IN HIM I TRUST [LEAN ON, RELY ON, and am CONFIDENT] in His Holy NAME. Let Your [STEADFAST] LOVINGKINDNESS, O LORD, be upon me, and in proportion I have hoped in You.

PSALM 36:5-10 (AMP)

Your LOVINGKINDNESS and GRA-CIOUSNESS for me, O LORD, extends to the skies. Your FAITHFULNESS to me [reaches] to the clouds. Your RIGH-TEOUSNESS is like the mountains of GOD, Your Judgments are like the great deep.

O LORD, You PRESERVE man and beast. How PRECIOUS is Your LOVINGKINDNESS toward me, O GOD! I take refuge in the shadow of Your wings.

I DRINK till I am FULL of Your ABUNDANCE...from the RIVER of YOUR DELIGHTS. For with You is the FOUNTAIN of DELIGHT [the foun-tain of LIFE-GIVING WATER]; in Your LIGHT I see LIGHT. O continue Your LOVINGKINDNESS and Your RIGHTEOUSNESS(SALVATION)to me....

PSALM 39:5-7 (AMP)

Behold, You have made my days as short as the width of my hand, And my lifetime is as nothing in Your sight. Surely, I am a mere breath [a wisp of smoke, a vapor that vanishes]!

Surely, I walk around like a shadow [in a charade]; surely I make an uproar for nothing; I build up riches, not knowing who will receive them. And now, LORD, for what do I EXPECTANTLY WAIT?

My HOPE [my CONFIDENT EXPECTATION] is IN YOU.

PSALM 40:4-9 (NLT)

I am [FORTUNATE, PROSPEROUS, and FAVORED by YOU, O GOD], because I TRUST in YOU. I have no confidence in the proud or those who lapse into lies.

Many, O LORD my GOD, are the WONDERFUL WORKS which You have done, and Your THOUGHTS toward me;

There is NONE to compare with You.

If I would declare and speak of your WONDERS, they would be TOO MANY TO COUNT.

Sacrifice and meal offering You do not desire, nor do You delight in them; You have OPENED my ears and given me the CAPACITY TO HEAR [and OBEY Your WORD];

Burnt offerings and sin offerings You do not require. Then I said, "Behold, I come [to the throne]; In the scroll of the book it is written of ME. I delight to do Your will, O my GOD; Your instructions are within my heart.

I have proclaimed Good News of RIGHTEOUSNESS [and the JOY that comes to me from OBEDIENCE to You] in the great assembly; behold, I will NOT RESTRAIN my LIPS [FROM PROCLAIMING YOUR RIGHTEOUSNESS], as You well know, O LORD.

PSALM 40:16 (AMP)

I REJOICE and am GLAD IN YOU;
I love YOUR SALVATION and I SAY
CONTINUALLY,
"THE LORD BE MAGNIFIED!"

Psalm 45:1-8 (NLT)

I will recite a lovely poem about the KING, for my tongue is like the pen of a skillful poet. You are the most HAND-SOME of ALL, GRACIOUS WORDS stream from your lips.

GOD Himself has blessed You forever.

Put on your sword, O mighty warrior!

You are so GLORIOUS, so MAJESTIC,

In your MAJESTY, ride out to VICTORY, DEFENDING TRUTH, HUMILITY, and JUSTICE.

Go forth to perform AWE-INSPIRING DEEDS! Your arrows are sharp, piercing Your enemies' hearts. The nations fall beneath Your feet.

Your throne, O GOD, ENDURES FOR-EVER and ever. You rule with a scepter of JUSTICE. You LOVE JUSTICE and HATE EVIL.

Therefore GOD, Your GOD, has anointed You, pouring out the OIL of JOY on You more than on anyone else.

Myrrh, aloes, and cassia perfume your robes. In ivory palaces the music of strings entertains You.

PSALMS 46:1-11 (AMP)

GOD is my REFUGE and STRENGTH [MIGHTY and IMPENETRABLE], a very present and well-proved HELP IN TROUBLE.

Therefore, I will NOT FEAR, though the earth should change and though the mountains be shaken and slip into the heart of the seas, though its waters roar and foam, though the mountains tremble at its roaring. There is a river whose streams make glad the city of GOD,

The Holy dwelling places of the MOST HIGH.

GOD is in the midst of her [His city], she will not be moved; GOD will help her when the morning dawns. The nations made an uproar, the kingdoms tottered and were moved;

He raised His voice, the earth melted.

The LORD of HOSTS are with me;

The GOD of Jacob is my STRONG-HOLD [my REFUGE, my HIGH TOWER].

I behold the works of the LORD,

Who has wrought desolations and wonders in the earth. He makes wars to cease to the end of the earth; He breaks the bow into pieces and snaps the spear in two; He burns the chariots with fire.

Be STILL and KNOW (RECOGNIZE, UNDERSTAND) that I AM GOD. I will be EXALTED among the nations! I will be EXALTED in the earth."

The LORD of HOSTS ARE WITH ME;

The GOD of Jacob is my STRONG-HOLD [my REFUGE, my HIGH TOWER].

PSALM 48:1-3 (AMP)

GREAT is the LORD, and GREATLY to be PRAISED, in the city of my GOD, His Holy mountain. Fair and beautiful in elevation, the joy of all the earth,

Is Mount Zion [the City of David] in the far north, The city of the great KING.

GOD, in her palaces, Has made Himself known as a STRONGHOLD.

PSALM 48:8-11 (AMP)

As I have heard, so have I seen

In the city of the LORD of HOSTS in the city of my GOD: GOD will establish her forever.

I have thought of Your LOVINGKIND-NESS, O GOD,

In the midst of Your temple

As is Your NAME , O GOD,

So is Your PRAISE to the ENDS OF THE EARTH; Your RIGHT HAND is FULL of RIGHTEOUSNESS (RIGHTNESS, JUSTICE).

Let Mount Zion be glad, let the daughters of Judah rejoice, because of Your [RIGHTEOUS] JUDGMENTS.

PSALM 50:1-6 (AMP)

The MIGHTY ONE, GOD, the LORD, has spoken. He has summoned the earth from the rising of the sun to its setting [from east to west]. Out of Zion, the perfection of beauty shines forth. Indeed, GOD has shone forth. May my GOD come and NOT KEEP SILENT.

Fire devours before Him, and around Him a mighty tempest rages. He summons the heavens above, and the earth, to JUDGE His people: "Gather My godly ones to Me, Those who have made a covenant with Me by sacrifice."

And the heavens declare His RIGHTEOUSNESS,

For GOD Himself is JUDGE.

PSALM 65 (NLT)

What mighty PRAISE, O GOD, belongs to you in Zion. I will fulfill my vows to you, for you answer my prayers. All of us must come to you. Though we are overwhelmed by our sins, you forgive them ALL. What joy for those you choose to bring near, those who live in your HOLY courts. What festivities await me inside your HOLY Temple.

You faithfully answer my prayers with AWESOME DEEDS, O God my SAVIOR. You are the HOPE of everyone on earth, even those who sail on distant seas.

You formed the mountains by your power and armed yourself with mighty strength.

You quieted the raging oceans with their pounding waves, and silenced the shouting of the nations.

Those who live at the ends of the earth stand in AWE of YOUR WONDERS.

From where the sun rises to where it sets, you inspire SHOUTS of JOY.

You take care of the earth and water it, making it rich and fertile. The river of GOD has plenty of water; it provides a bountiful harvest of grain, for you have ordered it so.

You drench the plowed ground with rain, melting the clods and leveling the ridges.

You soften the earth with showers, and bless its abundant crops. You crown the year with a bountiful harvest; even the hard pathways overflow with ABUNDANCE.

The grasslands of the wilderness become a lush pasture, and the hillsides BLOSSOM with JOY. The meadows are clothed with flocks of sheep, and the valleys are carpeted with grain. I SHOUT and SING FOR JOY!

PSALM 66:1-10 (AMP)

Shout JOYFULLY to GOD, all the earth;

Sing of the HONOR and GLORY and MAGNIFICENCE of His NAME.

Make His PRAISE GLORIOUS.

I say to GOD, "How AWESOME and FEARFULLY GLORIOUS are Your WORKS! Because of the GREATNESS of Your power, Your enemies will pretend to be obedient to You. All the earth will [bow down to] worship You [in SUBMISSIVE WONDER], and will sing PRAISES to You;

I will praise Your NAME in song."

I will say come and SEE the WORKS of GOD, He is AWESOME in His deeds toward me. He turned the sea into dry land; they crossed through the river on foot; there we rejoiced in Him.

Who rules by His MIGHT FOREVER, His eyes keep watch on the nations;

Do not let the rebellious exalt themselves.

I bless the LORD GOD...and make the sound of Your PRAISE be heard abroad,

You keep me among the living, and do not allow my feet to slip or stumble. For You have tested me, O GOD; You have refined me as silver is refined.

PSALM 67:1-7 (AMP)

GOD be GRACIOUS and KIND-HEARTED to me and bless me,

And make Your FACE shine [with favor] on me, that Your way may be known on earth, Your SALVATION and DELIVERANCE among all nations.

I PRAISE You, O GOD; let all the peoples PRAISE You. Let the nations be glad and sing for joy. For You will JUDGE the people FAIRLY and guide the nations on earth.

Let the peoples PRAISE You, O GOD;

Let all the peoples PRAISE You. The earth has yielded its harvest [as evidence of His approval]; GOD, my GOD, blesses me. GOD blesses me, and all the ends of the earth shall FEAR HIM [with AWE-INSPIRED REVERENCE and SUBMISSIVE WONDER].

PSALM 68:1-20 (AMP)

Let GOD arise, and His enemies be scattered; let those who hate Him flee before Him.

As smoke is driven away, so drive them away; as wax melts before the fire, so let the wicked and guilty perish before [the PRESENCE of] GOD.

But let the righteous be glad; I am in a good spirit before GOD. Yes, I rejoice with delight. I sing to GOD, I sing PRAISES to Your NAME; I lift up a song for You who rides through the desert—

Your NAME is the LORD—I am in a good spirit before You.

A FATHER of the fatherless and JUDGE and PROTECTOR of the widows, is GOD in His HOLY habitation. GOD makes a home for the lonely; He leads the prisoners into prosperity. Only the stubborn and rebellious dwell in a parched land.

O GOD, when You went out before Your people, when You marched through the wilderness, the earth trembled;

The heavens also poured down rain at the PRESENCE of GOD; Sinai itself trembled at the PRESENCE of GOD, the GOD of ISRAEL.

You, O GOD, sent abroad plentiful rain;

You confirmed Your inheritance when it was parched and weary. Your flock found a dwelling place in it; O GOD, in Your GOODNESS You provided for the poor.

The LORD gives the command [to take Canaan]; the women who proclaim the Good News are a great host (army);

"The kings of the [enemies'] armies flee, they flee, And the beautiful woman who remains at home divides the spoil [left behind]."

When you lie down [to rest] among the sheepfolds, you [Israel] are like the wings of a dove [of victory] overlaid with silver,

Its feathers glistening with gold [trophies taken from the enemy].

When the ALMIGHTY scattered [the Canaanite] kings in the land of Canaan,

It was snowing on Zalmon. A mountain of GOD is the mountain of Bashan; A [high] mountain of many summits is Mount Bashan [rising east of the Jordan].

Why do you look with envy, mountains with many peaks, at the mountain [of the city of Zion] which GOD has desired for His dwelling place?

Yes, the LORD will dwell there FOREVER. The chariots of GOD are myriads, thousands upon thousands; The LORD is among them as He was at Sinai, in HOLINESS.

You have ascended on high, You have led away captive Your captives; You have received gifts among men, even from the rebellious also, that the LORD GOD may dwell there.

BLESSED be the LORD, who bears my burden day by day, the GOD who is my SALVATION! GOD is to me a GOD of ACTS OF SALVATION; and to GOD belong escapes from death [setting me free].

PSALM 69:34-36 (AMP)

Let heaven and earth PRAISE Him,

The seas and everything that moves in them. For GOD will save Zion and rebuild the cities of Judah, that His servants may remain there and possess it. The descendants of His servants will inherit it,

And those who love His NAME will dwell in it.

PSALM 77:13-20 (AMP)

Your way, O God, is HOLY [far from sin and guilt].What god is great like our God?You are the [awesome] GOD who works [POWERFUL] WONDERS; You have demonstrated Your power among the people. You have with Your [GREAT] ARM redeemed Your people, The sons of Jacob and Joseph.

The waters [of the Red Sea] saw You, O GOD; the waters saw You, they were in anguish; the deeps also trembled. the clouds poured down water; the skies sent out a sound [of rumbling thunder]; Your arrows (lightning) flashed here and there.

The voice of Your thunder was in the whirlwind; the lightnings illumined the world; the earth trembled and shook.

Your way [of escape for Your people] was through the sea, and Your paths through the great waters, and Your footprints were not traceable. You led

*Your people like a flock by the hand
of Moses and Aaron [to the promised
goal].*

PSALM 84:10-12 (AMP)

For a day in Your courts is better than a thousand [anywhere else]; I would rather stand [as a doorkeeper] at the threshold of the house of my GOD, than to live [at ease] in the tents of wickedness.

For the LORD GOD is a sun and shield;

The LORD bestows GRACE and FAVOR and HONOR; no good thing will You withhold from me because I walk uprightly.

O LORD of HOSTS, I am blessed and GREATLY FAVORED, because I TRUST in You [I believe in You, rely on You, and commit myself to You with confident hope and EXPECTATION].

PSALM 85:10-13 (AMP)

Steadfast LOVE and TRUTH and FAITHFULNESS meet together;

RIGHTEOUSNESS and PEACE kiss each other. TRUTH springs from the earth, and RIGHTEOUSNESS looks down from heaven.

Indeed, the LORD will give what is GOOD, and our land will yield its produce. RIGHTEOUSNESS will go before Him and will make HIS FOOT-STEPS into a WAY [IN WHICH I WALK].

PSALM 87:1-3 (AMP)

His foundation is on the Holy mountain.

The LORD loves the gates of Zion More than all the dwellings of Jacob (Israel).

GLORIOUS things are spoken of you, O city of God [Jerusalem].

PSALM 89:9-18 (AMP)

You rule the swelling of the sea;
When its waves rise, You still them.

You have crushed Rahab (Egypt) like one who is slain; You have scattered Your enemies with Your MIGHTY ARM. The heavens are Yours, the earth also is Yours; the world and all that is in it, You have founded and established them.

The north and the south, You have created them; Mount Tabor and Mount Hermon SHOUT FOR JOY AT YOUR NAME. You have a STRONG ARM;

MIGHTY is Your hand, Your right hand is EXALTED.RIGHTEOUS-NESS and JUSTICE are the foundation of Your throne; LOVINGKINDNESS and TRUTH go before You.

I am blessed and happy because I know the joyful sound [of the trumpet's blast]!

I WALK, O LORD, IN the LIGHT and FAVOR of Your COUNTENANCE!

In Your NAME I REJOICE ALL the DAY, and in Your RIGHTEOUSNESS I am exalted. For You are the GLORY of my strength [my proud adornment], and by Your FAVOR my horn(strength) is exalted. For my shield belongs to the LORD, and our KING to the HOLY ONE OF ISRAEL.

PSALM 90:1-6 (AMP)

LORD, You have been [and are] our dwelling place [Our REFUGE, Our SANCTUARY, Our STABILITY] in all generations. Before the mountains were born, or before You had given birth to the earth and the world, even from everlasting to everlasting, You are [the ETERNAL] GOD.

You turn man back to dust, And say, "Return [to the earth], O children of [mortal] men!"

For a thousand years in Your sight, are like yesterday when it is past, or as a watch in the night. You have swept them away like a flood, they fall asleep [forgotten as soon as they are gone];

In the morning they are like grass which grows anew—in the morning it flourishes and springs up; in the evening it wilts and withers away.

PSALM 90:11-12 (AMP)

Who understands the power of Your anger? [Who connects this brevity of life among us with Your judgment of sin?]

And Your wrath, [who connects it] with the [REVERENT] FEAR that is due You?

So teach me to number my days, that I may cultivate and bring to You a heart of wisdom.

PSALM 91 (NLT)

I live in the shelter of the Most High and find rest in the Shadow of the Almighty. This I declare about the LORD:

He ALONE is my REFUGE, my place of SAFETY; He is my GOD, and I TRUST HIM!

For He will rescue me from EVERY trap and protect me from deadly DISEASE.

He will cover me with His feathers.

He will shelter me with His wings.

His faithful promises are my armor and PROTECTION.

Do NOT be AFRAID of the terrors of the night, nor the arrow that flies in the day.

Do not dread the DISEASE that stalks in darkness, nor the DISASTER that strikes at midday.

Though a thousand fall at my side,

though ten thousand are dying around me, these evils will not touch me. Just open your eyes, and see how the wicked are punished.

If I make the Lord my refuge, if I make the Most High my shelter, no evil will CONQUER me; no PLAGUE will come near my home. For He will order His angels to PROTECT me wherever I go.

They will hold me up with their hands so I won't even hurt my foot on a stone.

I will trample upon lions and cobras; I will crush fierce lions and serpents under my feet!

The LORD says, "I will RESCUE those who love me. I will PROTECT those who TRUST IN My NAME. When you CALL on me, I WILL ANSWER; I will be with you in trouble. I will RESCUE and HONOR you. I will REWARD you with a LONG LIFE and give you My SALVATION."

PSALM 93 (AMP)

The LORD REIGNS, He is CLOTHED with MAJESTY and SPLENDOR; The LORD has clothed and encircled Himself with STRENGTH; the world is firmly established, it cannot be moved.

Your throne is established from of old;

You are from everlasting. The floods have lifted up, O LORD. The floods have lifted up my voice; the floods lift up their pounding waves. More than the sounds of many waters. More than the mighty breakers of the sea.

The LORD on high is MIGHTY. Your precepts are fully confirmed and COMPLETELY RELIABLE;

HOLINESS adorns Your house, O LORD, forever.

PSALM 95:1-7 (AMP)

O come, let us sing to the LORD: I shout joyfully to the ROCK of our SALVATION. Let us come before His PRESENCE with a song of THANKSGIVING;

Let us shout joyfully to Him with songs.

For You, O LORD are a GREAT GOD

And a GREAT KING above all gods,

In whose hand are the depths of the earth;

The peaks of the mountains are Yours also. The sea is Yours, for You made it [by Your command]; and Your hands formed the dry land.

Let us come and WORSHIP and BOW DOWN, I kneel before the LORD my Maker [in REVERANT PRAISE and PRAYER].For He is my GOD and we are the sheep in His pasture and the sheep of His hand.

Psalm 96 (NLT)

Sing a new song to the LORD! Let the whole earth sing to the LORD! Sing to the LORD; PRAISE his NAME. Each day proclaim the Good News that he SAVES.

Publish his Glorious deeds among the nations. Tell everyone about the amazing things he does.

Great is the LORD!

He is most worthy of PRAISE! He is to be feared above all gods. The gods of other nations are mere idols, but the LORD made the heavens!

Honor and majesty surround Him; strength and beauty fill his sanctuary.

O nations of the world, recognize the LORD; recognize that the LORD is GLORIOUS and strong. Give to the LORD the GLORY He deserves!

Bring your offering and come into his courts.

WORSHIP the LORD in all his holy splendor. Let all the earth tremble before him. Tell all the nations, "The LORD reigns!" The world stands firm and cannot be shaken. He will JUDGE all peoples fairly.

Let the heavens be glad, and the earth rejoice! Let the sea and everything in it shout His PRAISE! Let the fields and their crops burst out with joy! Let the trees of the forest sing for joy before the LORD, for He is coming! He is coming to JUDGE the earth. He will JUDGE the world with JUSTICE, and the nations with His truth.

PSALM 97:1-12 (AMP)

The LORD REIGNS, let the earth rejoice; let the many islands and coastlands be glad. Clouds and thick darkness surround Him [as at Sinai];

RIGHTEOUSNESS and JUSTICE are the foundation of His throne. Fire goes before Him, and burns up His adversaries on all sides. His lightnings have illuminated the world; the earth has seen and trembled.

The mountains melted like wax at the PRESENCE of the LORD, at the PRESENCE of the LORD of the whole earth.

The heavens declare His RIGHTEOUSNESS, and all the peoples SEE His GLORY and BRILLIANCE.

Let all those be [deeply] ashamed who serve carved images, who boast in idols.

WORSHIP Him, all you gods! Zion heard this and was glad, and the daughters (cities) of Judah rejoiced [in relief] because of Your judgments, O LORD.

For You are the LORD MOST HIGH OVER ALL THE EARTH; You are EXALTED far above all gods.

You who love the LORD, HATE EVIL;

He PROTECTS the souls of His godly ones (believers), He RESCUES them from the hand of the wicked. LIGHT is sown [like seed] for the righteous and ILLUMINATES their path, and [irrepressible] JOY [is spread] for the upright in heart [who delight in His FAVOR and PROTECTION].

Rejoice in the LORD, you righteous ones [those whose moral and spiritual integrity places them in right standing with GOD],

And PRAISE and GIVE THANKS at the remembrance of His HOLY NAME.

PSALM 99:1-5 (AMP)

The LORD reigns, let the peoples tremble [with submissive wonder]!

He sits enthroned above the cherubim, let the earth shake! The LORD is GREAT in Zion, and He is EXALTED and MAGNIFIED above all the peoples.

Let them [REVERENTLY] PRAISE Your GREAT and AWESOME NAME; HOLY is He.

The strength of the KING loves JUSTICE and RIGHTEOUS JUDGMENT; You have established FAIRNESS; You have executed JUSTICE and RIGHTEOUSNESS in Jacob (Israel).

EXALT the LORD our GOD, And worship at His footstool; HOLY is He.

PSALM 103 (AMP)

I BLESS and affectionately PRAISE the LORD, O my soul, and ALL that is [DEEP] WITHIN ME, BLESS His HOLY NAME.

I BLESS and AFFECTIONALLY PRAISE the LORD, O my soul,

And I do not forget any of His benefits;

Who forgives ALL my sins, Who heals ALL my diseases; Who REDEEMS my life from the pit, He crowns me [lavishly] with LOVING KINDNESS and TENDER MERCY; He SATISFIES my years with GOOD THINGS, so that my YOUTH IS RENEWED like the [soaring] eagle.

The LORD executes RIGHTEOUSNESS and JUSTICE for all the oppressed. He made known His WAYS [of RIGHTEOUSNESS and JUSTICE] to Moses, His ACTS to the children of Israel.

The LORD is MERCIFUL and GRA-CIOUS, SLOW to ANGER and ABOUNDING COMPASSION and LOVINGKINDNESS.

He will not always strive with us, Nor will He keep His anger forever.

He has not dealt with me according to my sins [as I deserve], nor rewarded me [with punishment] according to my wickedness.

For as the heavens are high above the earth, so GREAT is His LOVINGKIND-NESS toward me because I FEAR and WORSHIP Him [with AWE-FILLED RESPECT and DEEPEST REVER-ENCE].

As far as the east is from the west, so far has He removed my transgressions from me. Just as a father loves his chil-dren, so, the LORD loves me because I FEAR and WORSHIP Him [with AWE-FILLED RESPECT and DEEP-EST REVERENCE].

For He knows my [mortal] frame; He remembers that I am [merely] dust. As for man, his days are like grass; like a flower of the field, so he flourishes. For the wind passes over it and it is no more, and its place knows it no longer. But the LOVINGKINDNESS of the LORD is from EVERLASTING to EVERLASTING on me because I [REVERENTLY] FEAR Him,

And His RIGHTEOUSNESS to my children's children, to those who honor and keep His covenant, and remember to do His commandments [imprinting His word on their hearts].

The LORD has established His throne in the heavens, His SOVEREIGNTY rules over all [the universe]. Bless the LORD, you His angels, You mighty ones who do His commandments, obey the voice of His WORD!

Bless the LORD, all you His hosts (armies of angels), you who serve Him and do His will. Bless the LORD, all you works

*of His, in all places of His dominion;
Bless and affectionately PRAISE the
LORD, O my soul!*

PSALM 104:1-34 (AMP)

Bless and AFFECTIONATELY PRAISE the LORD, O my soul! O LORD my GOD, You are VERY GREAT; You are clothed with SPLENDOR and MAJESTY,

[You are the One] who covers Yourself with LIGHT as with a garment, Who stretches out the heavens like a tent curtain, and lays the beams of His upper chambers in the waters [above the firmament].

Who makes the clouds His chariot, Who walks on the wings of the wind, and makes winds His messengers, Flames of FIRE His ministers.

He established the earth on its foundations, so, that it will not be moved forever and ever. You covered it with the deep as with a garment; the waters were standing above the mountains. At Your rebuke they fled; at the sound of Your thunder they hurried away.

The mountains rose, the valleys sank down to the place which You established for them. You set a boundary [for the waters] that they may not cross over, so that they will not return to cover the earth.

You send springs into the valleys; Their waters flow among the mountains. They give drink to every beast of the field; even the wild donkeys quench their thirst there. Beside them the birds of the heavens have their nests; they lift up their voices and sing among the branches.

He waters the mountains from His upper chambers; The earth is satisfied with the fruit of His works. He causes grass to grow for the cattle, and all that the earth produces for cultivation by man,

That man may bring food from the earth—wine to make the heart of man glad, oil to make his face glisten, and bread to sustain and strengthen man's heart.

The trees of the LORD drink their fill, the cedars of Lebanon which He has planted, where the birds make their nests;

As for the stork, the fir trees are her house. The high mountains are for the wild goats; The rocks are a refuge for the rock badgers.

He made the moon for the seasons; the sun knows the [exact] place of its setting.

You [O LORD] make darkness and it becomes night, in which prowls about every wild beast of the forest.

The young lions roar after their prey and seek their food from God. When the sun arises, they withdraw and lie down in their dens. Man goes out to his work and remains at his labor until evening. O LORD, how many and varied are Your works!

In WISDOM You have made them all;

the earth is full of Your riches and Your creatures. There is the sea, great and broad, in which are swarms without number; creatures both small and great.

There the ships [of the sea] sail, the Leviathan [the sea monster], which You formed play there. They all wait for You to give them their food in its appointed season.

You give it to them, they gather it up; You open Your hand, and they are filled and satisfied with GOOD [things]. You hide Your Face, they are dismayed; You take away their breath, they die, and return to their dust. You send out Your SPIRIT, they are created, You renew the face of the ground.

May the GLORY of the LORD endure Forever; may the LORD rejoice and be glad in His works—He looks at the earth, and it trembles; He touches the mountains, and they smoke.

*I will sing to the LORD as long as I live;
I will sing PRAISE to my GOD while I
have my being. May my meditation be
sweet and pleasing to You;*

*As for me, I will rejoice and be glad in
the LORD.*

PSALM 107:8-9 (AMP)

I give thanks to the LORD for His LOVINGKINDNESS, and for His WONDERFUL ACTS to the children of men! For He satisfies the parched throat, and fills the hungry appetite with what is GOOD.

PSALM 111:1-10 (AMP)

Praise the LORD! (Hallelujah!) I will give thanks to the LORD with All my heart, in the company of the upright and in the congregation. GREAT are the WORKS of the LORD,

Studied by all those who delight in them.

SPLENDID and MAJESTIC is His WORK, and His RIGHTEOUSNESS ENDURES FOREVER.

He has made His WONDERFUL ACTS to be REMEMBERED; the LORD is GRACIOUS and MERCIFUL and FULL of LOVING COMPASSION.

He has given food to those who fear Him [with AWE-INSPIRED REVERENCE];

He will remember His COVENANT FOREVER. He has declared and made known to His people the POWER of His WORKS, in giving them the heritage of the nations.

The WORKS of His hands are TRUTH and [ABSOLUTE] JUSTICE; ALL His PRECEPTS are SURE (ESTABLISHED, RELIABLE, TRUSTWORTHY).

They are upheld FOREVER and EVER;

They are done in [ABSOLUTE TRUTH]and UPRIGHTNESS.

He has sent REDEMPTION to me;

He has ordained His COVENANT FOREVER; HOLY and AWESOME is His NAME—[inspiring reverence and GODLY FEAR].

The [REVERENT] FEAR of the LORD is the BEGINNING (the PREREQUISITE , the ABSOLUTE ESSENTIAL , the ALPHABET) of WISDOM; A good understanding and a teachable heart are possessed by all those who do the will of the LORD; His PRAISE endures Forever.

PSALM 113 (AMP)

Praise the LORD! (Hallelujah!) Praise, O servants of the LORD, Praise the NAME of the LORD. Blessed be the NAME of the LORD from this time forth and forever. From the rising of the sun to its setting The NAME of the LORD is to be PRAISED [with AWE-INSPIRED REVERENCE].

The LORD is High above all nations, and His GLORY above the heavens. Who is like the LORD my GOD, Who is enthroned on high, Who humbles Himself to regard the heavens and the earth?

He raises the poor out of the dust, and lifts the needy from the ash heap, that He may seat them with princes, with the princes of His people. He makes the barren woman live in the house as a joyful mother of children.

PRAISE the LORD! (HALLELUJAH!)

PSALM 115:16-18 (AMP)

The heavens are the heavens of the LORD, But the earth He has given to the children of men. The dead do not PRAISE the LORD, nor do any who go down into silence; but as for me, I will BLESS and AFFECTIONATELY and GRATEFULLY PRAISE the LORD,

From this time forth and FOREVER.

PRAISE the LORD! (HALLELUJAH!)

PSALM 118:2-9 (AMP)

Oh let Israel say, "His LOVINGKIND-NESS ENDURES FOREVER." Oh let the house of Aaron say, "His LOVING-KINDNESS ENDURES FOREVER."

Oh let those who [reverently] fear the LORD, say, "His LOVINGKINDNESS ENDURES FOREVER." Out of my distress I called on the LORD; the LORD answered me and set me free.

The LORD is on my side; I will not fear.

What can [mere] man do to me? The LORD is on my side, He is among those who help me; therefore I will look [in triumph] on those who hate me.

It is better to take REFUGE in the LORD than to trust in man. It is better to take REFUGE in the LORD, Than to trust in princes.

PSALM 118:22-23 (AMP)

The STONE which the builders rejected
Has become the chief corner STONE.

This is from the LORD and is His doing;

It is marvelous in our eyes.

PSALM 121:1-5 (AMP)

I will lift up my eyes to the hills [of Jerusalem]—from where shall my help come? My help comes from the LORD, Who made heaven and earth.

He will not allow my foot to slip; He who keeps me will not slumber. Behold, He who keeps Israel will neither slumber [briefly] nor sleep [soundly]. The LORD is my keeper; the LORD is my shade on my right hand.

PSALM 121:7-8 (AMP)

The LORD will protect me from ALL evil; He will keep my life. The LORD will guard my going out and my coming in [Everything that I do] from this time forth and FOREVER.

PSALM 123:1-2 (AMP)

Unto you I lift up my eyes, O You who are enthroned in the heavens! Behold, as the eyes of servants look to the hand of their master, and as the eyes of a maid to the hand of her mistress, so, my eyes look to the LORD my GOD, until He is GRACIOUS and FAVORABLE toward me.

PSALM 126:1-3 (AMP)

When the LORD brought back the captives to Zion (Jerusalem), We were like those who dream [it seemed so unreal]. Then our mouth was filled with laughter, and our tongue with joyful shouting. Then they said among the nations, "The LORD has done GREAT things for them." The LORD has done GREAT things for me; I am glad!

PSALM 135:5-14 (AMP)

For I know that the LORD is GREAT and that my LORD is above all gods.

Whatever the LORD pleases, He does,

In the heavens and on the earth, in the seas and all deeps—Who causes the clouds to rise from the ends of the earth;

Who makes lightning for the rain,

And brings the wind from His storehouses; Who struck the firstborn of Egypt, both of man and animal;

Who sent signs and wonders into your midst, O Egypt, upon Pharaoh and all his servants.

Who struck many nations, and killed mighty kings, Sihon, king of the Amorites, Og, king of Bashan, and all the kingdoms of Canaan; and He gave their land as a heritage, a heritage to Israel His people.

Your NAME, O LORD, ENDURES FOREVER,

Your FAME and REMEMBRANCE,
O LORD, [ENDURES] throughout
ALL GENERATIONS.

For the LORD will JUDGE His people
And He will have COMPASSION on
His servants [revealing His MERCY].

PSALM 145:3-21 (AMP)

GREAT is the LORD, and Highly to be PRAISED, and His GREATNESS is [so vast and profound as to be] UNSEARCHABLE [INCOMPRE-HENSIBLE to man].

One generation shall PRAISE Your works to another, and shall declare Your MIGHTY and REMARKABLE

ACTS. On the GLORIOUS splendor of Your MAJESTY, and on Your WON-DERFUL WORKS, I will meditate.

People will speak of the power of Your AWESOME ACTS, and [with GRATI-TUDE and SUBMISSIVE WONDER] I will TELL of Your GREATNESS. I OVERFLOW [like a fountain] when I speak of Your GREAT and ABUN-DANT GOODNESS.

And will sing joyfully of Your RIGHTEOUSNESS.

The LORD is GRACIOUS and FULL of COMPASSION, SLOW

to ANGER and ABOUNDING in LOVING-KINDNESS.

The LORD is GOOD to ALL,

And His TENDER MERCIES are over ALL His WORKS [the entirety of things created].

All Your works shall give THANKS to You and PRAISE You, O LORD,

And Your godly ones will BLESS You.

They shall speak of the GLORY of YOUR KINGDOM, and talk of YOUR POWER, to make known to the sons of men Your MIGHTY ACTS

And the GLORIOUS MAJESTY of Your KINGDOM.

Your KINGDOM is an EVER-LASTING KINGDOM, and Your DOMINION ENDURES throughout all generations.

The LORD upholds all those [of His own] who fall, and raises up all those who are bowed down.

My eyes look to You [in HOPEFUL EXPECTATION], and You give me my food in due time. You open Your hand and satisfy the desire of every living thing.

The LORD is [UNWAVERINGLY] RIGHTEOUS in ALL His WAYS

And GRACIOUS and KIND in ALL His WORKS. The LORD is near to me when I call on Him, to all who call on Him in truth (without guile).

He will fulfill my desires because I FEAR and WORSHIP Him [with AWE-INSPIRED REVERENCE and OBEDIENCE]; He also will hear my cry and will SAVE me.

The LORD keeps me because I love Him,

But all the wicked He will destroy.

My mouth will speak the PRAISE of the LORD,

*And all flesh will bless and GRATE-
FULLY PRAISE His HOLY NAME
forever and ever.*

PSALM 146 (AMP)

PRAISE the LORD! (Hallelujah!)

PRAISE the LORD, O my soul!

While I live, I will PRAISE the LORD;

I will sing PRAISES to my GOD as long as I live.

I do not trust in princes, in mortal man, in whom there is no salvation (help).

When his spirit leaves him, he returns to the earth; in that very day his thoughts and plans perish. How BLESSED and GRACIOUSLY FAVORED am I because my GOD is the GOD of Jacob (Israel),

My HOPE is in the LORD my GOD,

Who made heaven and earth,

The sea, and all that is in them,

Who keeps truth and is FAITHFUL FOREVER, Who executes JUSTICE for the oppressed, Who gives food to the hungry.

The LORD sets free the prisoners.

The LORD opens the eyes of the blind;

The LORD lifts up those who are bowed down;

The LORD loves the righteous [the upright in heart].

The LORD protects the strangers;

He supports the fatherless and the widow;

But He makes crooked the way of the wicked.

The LORD shall REIGN FOREVER,

You are GOD, O Zion, to all generations.

PRAISE the LORD! (HALLELUJAH!)

PSALM 147 (AMP)

PRAISE the LORD!

For it is GOOD to sing PRAISES to our [GRACIOUS and MAJESTIC] GOD;

PRAISE is becoming and appropriate.

The LORD is building up Jerusalem;

He is gathering [together] the exiles of Israel. He heals the brokenhearted and binds up their wounds [healing their pain and comforting their sorrow].

He counts the number of the stars; He calls them all by their names. GREAT is our [MAJESTIC and MIGHTY] LORD and ABUNDANT in STRENGTH;

His UNDERSTANDING is INEX-HAUSTIBLE [infinite, boundless].

The LORD lifts up the humble; He casts the wicked down to the ground. Sing to the LORD with THANKSGIVING; Sing PRAISES to our GOD with the lyre,

Who covers the heavens with clouds,

Who provides rain for the earth, Who makes grass grow on the mountains.

He gives to the beast its food,

And to the young ravens that for which they cry.

He does not delight in the strength (military power) of the horse, nor does He take pleasure in the legs (strength) of a man. The LORD favors those who FEAR and WORSHIP Him [with AWE-INSPIRED REVERENCE and OBEDIENCE], those who WAIT for His MERCY and LOVINGKINDNESS.

PRAISE the LORD, O Jerusalem!

PRAISE your GOD, O Zion!

For He has strengthened the bars of my gates,

He has blessed my children within me.

He makes peace in my borders;

He satisfies me with the finest of the wheat.

He sends His command to the earth;

His WORD runs very swiftly.

He gives [to the earth] snow like [a blanket of] wool;

He scatters the frost like ashes.

He casts out His ice like fragments;

Who can stand before His cold?

He sends out His WORD and melts the ice;

He causes His wind to blow and the waters to flow.

He declares His WORD to Jacob,

His statutes and His ordinances to Israel.

He has not dealt this way with any [other] nation;

They have not known [understood, appreciated, heeded, or cherished] His ordinances.

PRAISE the LORD! (HALLELUJAH!)

ABOUT
FELIX HALPERN

Felix Halpern was born in 1952 in the Netherlands. As a child his family immigrated to the United States, where he was raised in the northern New Jersey area. Prior to full-time ministry, he established a lucrative career in the precious metals and diamond industries located in the International Diamond Center of New York City. Immersed for nearly two decades in the Orthodox and Hassidic Jewish communities, he understands well the heart of the Jewish people.

Coming from a rich Jewish heritage, he is also rooted in Nazi resistance. Rabbi Halpern's paternal grandfather was an Orthodox rabbi and leader of his own synagogue in Germany, and his maternal grandparents established one of the many underground resistance movements against Hitler throughout the Netherlands. It is also where his father received the knowledge and understanding of his Messiah while being hidden with other Jews, after miraculously escaping Germany.

Ministry Today

Today, Felix Halpern ministers nationally and internationally with a message of restoration between Jew and Gentile and a strong burden to bring the Father's love to the nations.

Felix Halpern serves as a nationally appointed missionary to the Jewish people, and for twenty years he and his wife Bonnie served as senior leaders of a Messianic congregation that they founded, Beth Chofesh (House of Freedom).

He pioneered the first National Jewish Fellowship of the Assemblies of God and has served the first four years as its president. He has also served as a general presbyter for the Assemblies of God, on the AG Board of Ethnicity, and also on the board of Lost Lamb Evangelistic Association.

In 2013 God provided the means to form the first Resource Office for Jewish Ministry within the Assemblies of God in the greater New York and New Jersey metropolitan region, called Metro Jewish Resources.

In 2019, out of his life and death experience and his journey into the third heaven, Chofesh Ministries (Freedom Ministries) was formed in 2020.

For more information:

Felix Halpern

PO Box 3777

Wayne, NJ 07470

Phone: 973-461-9786

Email: hisglobalglory@gmail.co

Web: www.chofesh.org